First published in Great Britain in 2007 by Buster Books,
an imprint of Michael O'Mara Books Limited,
9 Lion Yard, Tremadoc Road, London SW4 7NQ

Written by Jenny Siklos
Illustrated by Ruth Galloway
Created and produced by The Complete Works
St Mary's Road, Royal Leamington Spa, Warwickshire CV31 1JP

A CIP catalogue record for this book is available from the British Library

ISBN: 978-1-906082-03-1

2 4 6 8 10 9 7 5 3 1

www.mombooks.com/busterbooks

Printed and bound in Italy by L.E.G.O.

Papers used by Buster Books are natural, recyclable products made from wood grown in sustainable forests. The manufacturing processes conform to the environmental regulations of the country of origin.

The BOYS' Annual 2008

Buster Books

CONTENTS

Quizzes & Puzzles

Outdoor Stuff

Fun Facts

Did You Know?

Songs & Stories

IT'S A...
BOYS' WORLD

There are boys all over the world that are a lot like you. They may use different words, but they all speak the same language – *boy*! Here's a quiz to see how much you know about your international brothers. You'll find the answers on page 60.

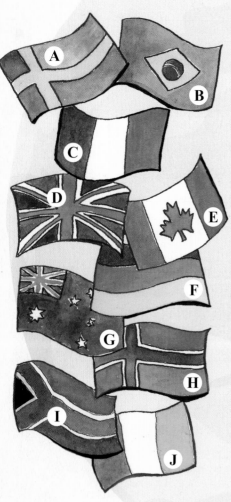

1. Which country has a whole day's holiday devoted to boys?
a) Germany b) Iran c) Japan d) USA

2. In which language does 'pojke' mean boy?
a) Polish b) Russian c) Swedish d) Zulu

3. In which country do boys race horses at the age of five, or younger?
a) Mongolia b) Norway c) Peru d) Taiwan

4. In which country do boys train and work with elephants for the whole of their lives?
a) India b) Italy c) Mexico d) Zimbabwe

5. In which country do many boys spend time as a novice Buddhist monk?
a) China b) Finland c) Germany d) Thailand

6. Which country has more boys than girls?
a) Chile b) China c) Jamaica d) Mexico

7. Which country introduced baseball caps to the world?
a) China b) Greece c) Spain d) USA

8. In which country did the youngest-ever bullfighter live?
a) Cuba b) Mexico c) Norway d) Spain

9. In which country do boys spend much of their childhoods in a kayak (canoe)?
a) Bahamas b) Greenland c) Iceland d) Spain

FLAG FLURRY
Here's a chance to test your knowledge of flags around the world.
Try to match as many country names as you can to the flags above. Answers on page 60.

COUNTRY NAMES
1. South Africa **2.** Ireland **3.** Canada **4.** Sweden **5.** China **6.** USA **7.** France
8. Great Britain **9.** Israel **10.** Germany **11.** Brazil **12.** Switzerland **13.** Italy **14.** Norway
15. Jamaica **16.** Greece **17.** Australia **18.** Spain **19.** Japan **20.** Ukraine

JOKE TIME

PUT YOUR HANDS UP

Boys love to make up cool ways to communicate with one another. Through hand gestures, boys can 'talk' without even opening their mouths. Here's a guide to some of the best-known gestures and what they mean.

HE'S BONKERS

Useful for pointing out to others that someone they are speaking to isn't quite all there. However, in Argentina, it means, 'You've got a phone call'.

EVERYTHING'S FINE

This gesture shows your friends that everything is fine and all right. But if you're in Italy, this sign means that someone's an idiot.

YO, BRO

Lots of cool boys tap clenched fists as a greeting.

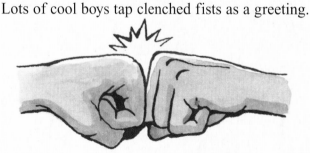

WICKED

Many boys make this gesture when someone does something cool, or when they are happy. Don't use this on holiday though, as in some countries it's rude.

WELL DONE

This thumbs-up gesture is very popular in a lot of countries. Boys use it when they are congratulating someone.

HIGH FIVE

Great for congratulating team mates and friends on a job well done. In the USA, there are low fives and sideways fives.

DID YOU KNOW?

Positive hand gestures are usually made with the palm side facing towards the person you're communicating with, such as waving hello to a mate. Negative ones often show the back of your hand, such as waving a clenched fist with your thumb facing in.

SURVIVAL GUIDE

• PART ONE •

If you can light a campfire, know where to store food safely and can read a map, you're a boy that others will look up to as a natural leader. But if you can't and need some tips, keep reading.

LIGHTING A FIRE

1. First, make sure campfires are allowed where you have chosen to camp. You don't want to get caught by a fire warden.
2. If it's allowed, collect some tinder (dry leaves, bark, or paper) and some kindling (twigs and small sticks).

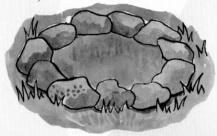

3. Away from trees or bushes, clear the ground and make a circle of rocks – this is known as a 'fire ring'. It will help contain your fire's ashes.

4. Start with the tinder and make a small pile in the centre of the fire ring.
5. Build a teepee of kindling around the tinder, a few layers thick. Don't make the kindling too thick, as air needs to circulate for the fire to burn. Make sure you keep the shape of the teepee.
6. Light the tinder from the bottom of the teepee, as flames burn upwards. The tinder will be easier to light than the kindling.
7. As the fire begins to grow, add more kindling until it's burning well.
8. Then add some larger branches and enjoy.

• SAFETY TIPS •

• Never use charcoal, petrol or paraffin on your fire. • To start the fire, an adult should use either matches or a lighter. • Don't burn 'green' wood, as it has too much sap in it. It'll just burn slowly and make alarming popping sounds. • Never cut wood from any trees that are still standing. • Don't start a fire on a hill, as fire travels uphill fast. • Never start a fire when it's very windy. • Never leave a fire unattended, or allow it to grow into a bonfire.

KEEPING FOOD SAFE

• *Never* take food into your tent for the night. Animals will find it and by finding it, they'll find you!

• Try and keep your food in containers. These make it impossible for animals to smell food because they're airtight and keep odours in.

• If you don't have any containers, hang your food in pouches, strung up high from a tree branch.

• Fill two pouches with food supplies and attach the end of a rope to each pouch. You do this to balance the pouches as they hang.

• Use a pole, or a long branch, to hang the pouches on a branch, as shown below.

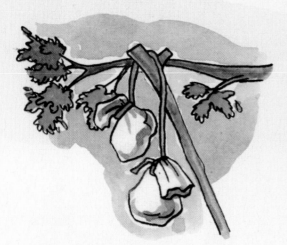

• Sometimes, animals still manage to get at your food, so you might have to go outside your tent and scare them off with a lot of noise.

BEATING ANNOYING INSECTS

Many insects can be annoying. Lighting a citronella candle will help, as insects don't like the smell.

A lot of insects also don't like smoke, so you should find you have fewer insects around when your campfire is burning.

> • **WARNING** •
> Remember, do *not* take candles
> into your tent – it might catch fire!

Other ways to avoid insects are by rubbing the inside of an orange peel on your arms, legs and face, and wearing dark-coloured clothes with long sleeves.

Lastly, avoid camping near still water – the favourite hangout of mosquitoes.

BATS AND DRAGONFLIES

Don't be scared if bats and dragonflies swoop over your campsite. This is a good thing, as these creatures love to eat mosquitoes and other nasty flying insects.

HOW TO MAKE 'SMORES'

These are a delicious campfire treat.

You will need: some plain biscuits / bars of chocolate / large marshmallows / long, thin sticks that have been soaked in water, or skewers of some kind.

1. Take two biscuits and lay some chocolate on to one of them.

2. Once your fire is going well, pop two marshmallows onto a stick.

3. Hold the stick slightly over the flames. Some people like the marshmallows to catch fire a little. Others prefer to let the marshmallows get golden brown. If they catch fire, blow them out quickly, or they'll turn into melted goo and plop into the fire.

4. When the marshmallows are soft, place them with the stick still inside onto one of the biscuits. Make a sandwich with the other biscuit. Squeeze the biscuits together and slide the stick out. Eat and enjoy.

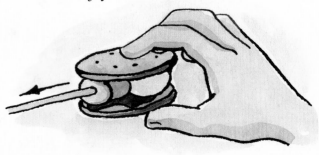

• WARNING •

The marshmallows are going to be *very* hot, so be extremely careful that you don't burn your fingers, or your tongue.

CAMPFIRE SONGS & STORIES

There's a lot to be said for singing and telling campfire songs and stories under the stars. It brings everyone together. It also allows you to sing and tell gross songs and stories that you would normally get into trouble for telling! Here's a quick song for you to try.

MY SPLATTERED DOG, GROVER

I'm stepping over my splattered Grover,
That I ran over with Dad's new mower.
One leg is twisted, the other has gone,
The third one is sprinkled all over the lawn.
Can't start explaining the one remaining,
It's stuck to the garage door.
I'm stepping over poor old Grover,
That I ran over with Dad's new mower.

You can also have lots of fun telling dumb stories and getting everyone to make the appropriate hand gestures to go with the story. Here's an example.

I brought a baby bumble bee home. Mummy* was so proud. I brought a baby bumble bee home. Oh, no! My baby bumble bee just stung my hand!

I squashed up my naughty bumble bee. Mummy* was so proud. I'm squashing my baby bumble bee right up. Oh, no! It's all over my hands!

I licked my baby bumble bee off my hands. Mummy* was proud. I licked my baby bumble bee right off my hands. Oh, no! I think I'm going to be sick!

I puked up my baby bumble bee now. Mummy* was so proud. I puked my baby bumble bee right up. Oh, no! It made a terrible mess!

I've mopped up my baby bumble bee now. Won't my Mummy* be proud? I've mopped my baby bumble bee right up. Mummy*, are you proud?

* can be substituted with any other family member

HAND GESTURES - PART 1

Cup your hands together, as if you were carrying a captured bee and walk on the spot, until you get to 'Oh, no!' Now stop all movement and emphasise the statement with an appropriate, 'I've been stung,' expression.

PART 4

Now pretend you're being sick! Exaggerate the stomach movements as much as possible.

PART 2

Mash your hands together, as though you're squashing the bee.

PART 3

While talking, pretend to lick your hands. Keep them flat and move them with a sweeping motion in front of your mouth.

PART 5

With a pretend mop in your hands, mop the ground as though you're cleaning up the sick.

FLICK THIS!

It's time to find the artist in you and get him drawing a flick book. Before you know it, you will have created an animated short 'film' using nothing more high-tech than a notebook, a pencil and some marker pens.

You will need: a small notebook, (preferably long and narrow) / a pencil / some coloured marker pens.

STICK MAN FLICK BOOK

1. Start by drawing a stick man on the last page of your notebook.

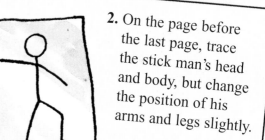

2. On the page before the last page, trace the stick man's head and body, but change the position of his arms and legs slightly.

3. Trace that drawing onto the next page, but again, position the man slightly differently.

4. When you've drawn on all the pages, flick the book from back to front and watch your man move about. With practice, you can make a stick man run across the pages, turn cartwheels and dance about.

JOKE TIME

Q. Why do birds fly south in the Winter?
A. Because it is too far to walk!

DID YOU KNOW?

The flick book works on the idea of 'persistence of vision' and is a basic kind of animation that works on the same principle as a movie. The human eye can only remember an image for a split second. As you flick through the book, the eye takes each separate image and 'links' them together. The German word for flick book is 'daumenkino', which means 'thumb cinema'.

FLICK BOOK IDEAS

After you've mastered the stick man, try these…

ONE SIDE TO THE OTHER

Make a character move from one side of your flick book and disappear on the other side, as shown in this series of drawings.

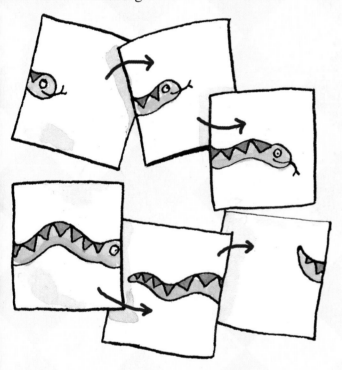

FAR AWAY TO CLOSE UP

Start with your character very far away. Then make it slowly approach, ending up with a huge close up. This is especially effective with scary things, such as dinosaurs.

CHOMP! CHOMP!

Lots of flick books like to focus on one character making another character disappear in some way – usually by being eaten! Try creating a fishy flick book. Start with one small fish being eaten by a bigger fish, that gets eaten by a bigger fish, that gets eaten by a bigger fish and so on.

WAYS TO ANNOY YOUR BROTHER OR SISTER

Many boys experience the 'joys' of having a brother or a sister – a 'sibling'. This includes the joy of sharing a bedroom with another person and the joy of listening to them whine endlessly on the phone for hours. So, if you find your sibling really joyless and annoying, here's how you can get one up on them.

PUT PLASTIC WRAP ON THE TOILET SEAT

When your sibling gets up in the middle of the night because 'nature' is calling, 'nature' will go all over the floor, instead of down the toilet.

PUT A 'PLEASE IGNORE ME' SIGN ON THEIR BACK

Your sibling will talk to people and grow more frustrated with every passing minute, as they are completely ignored and don't know why.

PLEASE IGNORE ME

PLAY 'WAKEY-WAKEY'

Gather as many alarm clocks as you can and hide them around your sibling's bedroom. Make sure you set them to different times. Your sibling will go mad trying to find them all.

MAKE AN IRRITATING SOUND

Make an annoying, high-pitched repetitive sound. Follow your sibling around the house as you do it, getting louder and louder, and watch as their annoyance grows.

BE A COPY CAT

Repeat whatever your sibling says, paying close attention to their intonation (the rise and fall of their voice). For even more fun, copy their movements and gestures, too.

PUT JAM ON THEIR BEDROOM DOOR HANDLE

Your sibling will get really cross and sticky, as they try to open their bedroom door and can't.

TRICK THEM

Very carefully glue some coins to an old plate and let them dry. Then place the plate somewhere in your house. When your sibling spots the coins, enjoy watching them break their nails and fingers trying to pick up the coins.

PUZZLED?

Feeling relaxed? See how well you do with these puzzles. All answers can be found on page 60.

ROAD RAGE

The picture below has exploded into 20 pieces. Can you put it back together again? See if you can match each numbered piece to its correct lettered position.

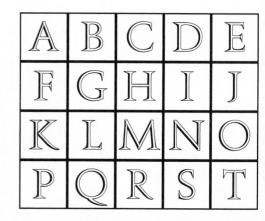

A	B	C	D	E
F	G	H	I	J
K	L	M	N	O
P	Q	R	S	T

1

2

3

4

5

6

7

8

9

10

11

12

13

14

15

16

17

18

19

20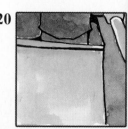

A WORM 'WRIDDLE'

This garden has been taken over by worms!
How many worms can you find?

BRAIN-ACHE

A milkman has two empty jugs – a three litre jug and a five litre jug. How can he measure out exactly two litres of milk without wasting any?

That 'Brain-Ache' was easy! Here's a much harder one. See how you do with this one.

A milkman has two empty jugs – a three litre jug and a five litre jug. How can he measure exactly one litre of milk without wasting any?

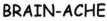

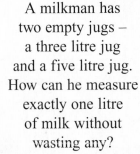

IT'S A RIDDLE

Below are the lyrics of a traditional folk song. Can you work out how these things are possible?

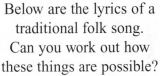

I gave my love a cherry
That had no stone.
I gave my love a chicken
That had no bone.
I told my love a story
That had no end.
I gave my love a baby
With no crying.

How can there be a cherry
That has no stone?
And how can there be a chicken
That has no bone?
And how can there be a story
That has no end?
And how can there be a baby
With no crying?

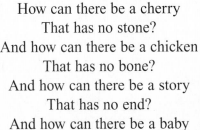

WILDLIFE WATCH

As animals lose more and more of their habitats, gardens are playing a bigger role as safe havens for a variety of creatures. Food, water and nesting sites are all necessary to create a diverse habitat for a wide variety of garden wildlife. Here's a quick guide to help make your garden visitors feel safe and contented.

BUTTERFLIES, MOTHS AND BUMBLE BEES

These flying insects are lots of fun to watch. Butterflies are attracted to blue, white and yellow flowers – these are the colours they prefer. Encourage your parents to plant Buddleia, Valerian and Sweet William – butterflies love their nectar.

Moths like strong-scented plants with pale colours, such as Jasmine flowers, Madonna Lilies, Evening Primroses and the exotic Yucca plant.

Bumble bees like the colours blue, lavender, purple and white. Try and make sure there are lots of Snapdragons, Sweet Peas and Heliotropes in your garden.

FROGS, TOADS AND NEWTS

Putting a pond in your garden will provide frogs, toads and newts with a much-needed habitat. Don't worry if these animals don't show up in your pond overnight. They, and a host of interesting insects, should eventually discover your pond.

To help your frogs get through the winter months, make sure your pond is 60–90 cm deep at some point, so that they can dig down into the mud to overwinter. The depth is important, so that they don't freeze.

In spring and summer, even a small garden pond might have over a hundred newts in it.

JOKE TIME

Q. What is worse than finding a worm
in your apple?
A. Finding half a worm in your apple!

GARDEN BIRDS

A good way to attract a variety of birds like
Blue Tits, Great Tits, Wagtails and Robins, is by
having a nesting box, which you can get from
most good garden centres. But make sure…

… your nesting box has small drain holes
in the bottom to let rainwater out.

… it is out of the reach of cats and mice.

… that if it has a hinged lid, it is securely
fastened, otherwise magpies and
squirrels might get in.

… it is not painted on the inside. Leave it
unfinished, so birds don't peck at it and
eat the paint, which may harm them.

… it doesn't have a perch attached to it,
as this will give predator birds a place from
which to intimidate the nesting birds.

… you put the box up well before spring.
This will increase your chances of
getting a pair of birds to nest in it that year.
If you don't get any nesting birds,
keep the box up, as other birds might use
it as a roost during winter.

THE WILD SIDE

Letting the grass grow
and planting wild flowers
in a patch of your garden
will attract lots of wildlife.
It might not look that tidy,
but your mum and dad
will forget that when
they see lots of lovely
butterflies fluttering
about. You might even
end up attracting other
sorts of wildlife.

BOOM-BANG-A-BANG!

Bicarbonate of soda is not a boring, average, everyday substance. You can have fun with it and learn something about chemistry at the same time.

WATCH THIS MOUNTAIN BLOW

To make a papier-mâché volcano and stage some amazing eruptions, you will need: PVA glue / warm water / a spoon / a bowl / some strips of newspaper, each about 2 cm wide / 1 plastic bottle, 20 cm tall / a square of cardboard, 60 cm x 60 cm / masking tape / paint and a paint brush / 1 cup of vinegar / red food colouring / 4 tablespoons of bicarbonate of soda.

1. First, prepare the papier-mâché paste. Mix two parts of glue to one part of water and stir well.
2. Dip the newspaper strips into the mixture and let the mixture soak into them completely. Put the mixture and strips to one side.
3. Now you can start putting together the base of the volcano. First, place the bottle in the centre of the cardboard square.
4. Then attach strips of masking tape from the top of the bottle to different points near the edge of the cardboard. Keep adding strips until your bottle is upright and very secure.

5. Pick up the newspaper strips, one at a time. Run them between two fingers to take off any excess paste. Now drape them across the masking tape strips. Be careful not to cover the opening of the bottle.

6. When the volcano is covered, let it dry overnight.
7. When dry, paint it. Why not add toy dinosaurs, or palm trees to the base of your volcano to give it a prehistoric feel?

JOKE TIME

Q. What's the best thing to give a seasick whale?
A. Plenty of room!

Now gather all your friends to watch the eruption.

1. Pour the vinegar into the bottle's opening – the 'mouth' of the volcano.
2. Drop in ten drops of food colouring.
3. Pour in all the bicarbonate of soda very quickly. Step back and enjoy the foamy eruption.

WHAT MAKES THE FOAM?

You're seeing some basic chemistry in action here. You have an acid (vinegar) reacting with a base (bicarbonate of soda). When they react with each other, bubbles of carbon dioxide gas are released. This is what makes the volcano foam.

PENNIES FOR YOUR THOUGHTS

Here's a simple experiment you can do with a few copper coins. You will need: 3 tablespoons of white vinegar / 1 shallow bowl / 1 teaspoon of salt / a spoon / 20 dull copper coins / paper towels / water.

1. Pour the vinegar into the bowl and add the salt. Stir the solution until the salt has dissolved.
2. Now put all the pennies into the solution and leave them there for about five minutes.
3. After five minutes, remove ten of the pennies from the liquid and place them on a paper towel.
4. Then remove the ten leftover pennies from the solution, but this time, rinse them under running water. Place the rinsed pennies on a separate paper towel.
5. Wait about an hour and take a look at the two sets of coins. What has happened to them? You'll find the explanation on page 60.

CRACK THAT ¬ π ø √ * & @ ! • ∆ ^ CODE

If you want to send your mates a message, but not let anyone else read it, the best thing to do is make up a code.

A secret code can be anything you want it to be. One simple code is to shift letters. For example, if you make B stand for A, C stand for B and so on, then BAD would be written as CBE.

For another code, you could reverse the alphabet. For example, the sequence ABCDE would be written as ZYXWV, so BAD would be YZW.

A	=	B	N	=	O		
B	=	C	O	=	P		
C	=	D	P	=	Q		
D	=	E	Q	=	R		
E	=	F	R	=	S		
F	=	G	S	=	T		
G	=	H	T	=	U		
H	=	I	U	=	V		
I	=	J	V	=	W		
J	=	K	W	=	X		
K	=	L	X	=	Y		
L	=	M	Y	=	Z		
M	=	N	Z	=	A		

A	=	Z	N	=	M
B	=	Y	O	=	L
C	=	X	P	=	K
D	=	W	Q	=	J
E	=	V	R	=	I
F	=	U	S	=	H
G	=	T	T	=	G
H	=	S	U	=	F
I	=	R	V	=	E
J	=	Q	W	=	D
K	=	P	X	=	C
L	=	O	Y	=	B
M	=	N	Z	=	A

Using the code above, see if you can work out what this message is.

TP, ZPV UIJOL ZPV DBO DSBDL UIJT POF, DMFWFS DMPHT?

What do you think this message is? All answers can be found on page 60.

GSZG LMV DZH VZHB, GSRH LMV RH NFXS SZIWVI.

You can also try replacing letters with numbers, symbols and coloured dots.

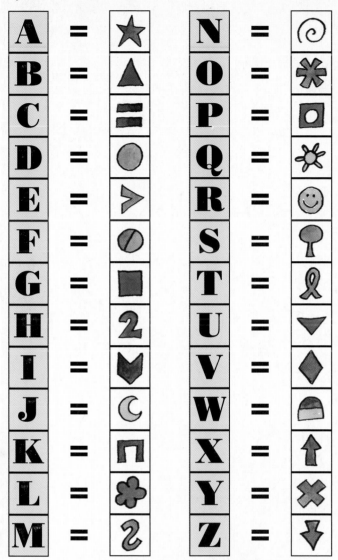

Using the code above, see if you can send your friends some secret messages.

INVISIBLE INK

If you want to keep your messages really secret, the best thing to do is write them in invisible ink! You will need: a paint brush / some lemon juice / some paper.

Dip your paint brush in the lemon juice. Then write, or draw something on the paper and leave it to dry.

To see the message, simply heat the paper up. *Very* carefully, hold the paper close to a lit 60 watt bulb. Gradually, the image will appear. Don't rest the paper on the bulb, or it may catch fire.

• WARNING •

Remember, you *must* keep your fingers away from the bulb – it will be *very* hot!

BET YOU CAN'T DO THIS

As a boy, you should have several utterly useless, but nonetheless fun, skills you can call upon.

SPIN A BALL ON YOUR FINGER

This trick impresses people. It's strangely elegant and the more you do it, the better you will become at it.

1. If you are right-handed, balance a ball on the pads of the five fingers of your right hand. Balance it on your left hand if you are left-handed.

2. Stretch your arm out until your elbow is slightly bent.

3. Flick your wrist quickly to the left if you are holding the ball with your right hand, to the right if you are using your left hand, while you bend your elbow 90 degrees. The ball should flick up and jump to your fingertips for a split second. Immediately bend your other fingers and let the ball spin on just your middle finger.

4. Keep the ball spinning by lightly tapping it in the direction it's spinning with the fingers of your other hand. Remember, practice makes perfect!

DID YOU KNOW?

The world record for the longest time spent spinning a basketball on a finger is 4 hours 15 minutes.

HOW TO DO 'KEEPIE-UPPIES'

Doing 'Keepie-Uppies' is a great way to practise your football skills. All you need is a ball. It's also a good way to get warmed up before playing or to improve your 'touch' with the ball.

1. Find a flat surface, such as a driveway.
2. Hold the ball above one of your feet.

3. Drop the ball onto your foot and kick your foot up a little as the ball lands on it. Not too much, as that makes the ball fly up into the air, but just enough that you can catch the ball with your hands when it's in the air.

4. Do this over and over again with each foot.
5. Next, try to do it twice in a row. Don't catch the ball, just let it fall back onto your foot and bounce it up again. Then try to kick the ball up as many times as you can without it touching the ground.

WHISTLE THROUGH YOUR FINGERS

You've probably heard someone do this, perhaps while hailing a taxi, or trying to get a person's attention.

1. Place the tips of your thumb and index finger together.

3. With your fingertips on the tip of your tongue, push your tongue slightly back and upwards until your lips close on your top knuckle. Practise this while looking in a mirror.
4. Tighten your lips over your fingers and teeth until the only opening is in the V between the ends of your fingers. This is the hardest part to get right.

2. Then place them into your mouth at an angle, as shown. The proper angle differs from person to person. You'll probably need to experiment a bit to find the right position.

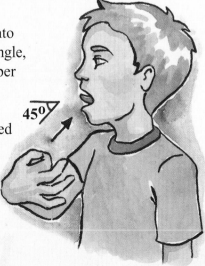

45°

5. Blow out steadily. You'll need to adjust the position of your fingers, tongue and lips until you produce a fabulously shrill, shrieking whistle.

WORMERY, SWEET WORMERY

Worms are the world's most efficient recyclers. A wormery will reduce your kitchen rubbish and keep your mum and dad happy with loads of organic compost for the garden.

HOW TO MAKE A WORMERY

1. BUILD A HOME FOR WORMS

You can use an old plastic dustbin, but it must have several 2 mm holes (25 cm apart) at the bottom, so water can escape and air can circulate inside. If you don't add the holes, the worms will stay at the bottom of the bin and could drown. The deepest your bin can be is 60 cm, because composting worms don't go deeper than that. The bin needs a cover to keep the light out and to prevent the compost from drying out.

2. PREPARE THE BIN

Fill your bin with thin strips of unbleached, corrugated cardboard, or shredded newspaper, straw, dry grass or other similar material. This provides a source of fibre for the worms to eat and keeps the bin well-ventilated. Sprinkle a light layer of soil on top and thoroughly moisten. Allow the water to soak in for at least a day before adding the worms.

DID YOU KNOW?

• Worms can live an amazingly long time. For example, an earthworm can live up to 6 years.
• The Dutch have outlawed using earthworms for fishing bait.
• An earthworm's poo is called a 'casting'. A 'midden' is a mound of leaves held down by the worm's castings. Worms put these over the entrances to their burrows.
• Earthworms eat twice their own body weight each day.

3. BUY AT LEAST A HUNDRED WORMS

The internet, or a local fishing supply shop are good places to find worms. Although you can just dig up earthworms from your garden, it's not recommended, as those worms aren't suited to wormeries.

Once you buy your first batch, you shouldn't have to buy any more, as they breed very quickly.

Good worms to try are…

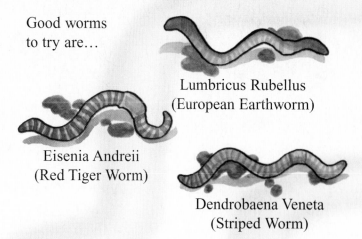

Lumbricus Rubellus
(European Earthworm)

Eisenia Andreii
(Red Tiger Worm)

Dendrobaena Veneta
(Striped Worm)

4. LOOK AFTER YOUR BIN

Keep your bin off the ground on some bricks, as this will help speed composting and keep your worms happy.

A light near the wormery will help to ensure your worms stay inside the bin. Worms don't like light and will avoid it, preferring the darkness of the bin.

With a spray bottle, mist the surface soil of the wormery with water every other day, so that the worms don't dry out.

Feed your worms leftover vegetable scraps and peelings at least once a week. Your worms will eat everything in your bin quickly and you will soon need to add more fibrous material.

5. COLLECT THE COMPOST

Making compost can take six to eight weeks, sometimes it can take up to a year. Keep an eye on your bin and when most of the waste has broken down, put on some rubber gloves and remove any large uncomposted vegetable matter and put this to one side. Then, gently scoop some of the worms and compost mixture onto a piece of newspaper. Separate the compost carefully. If you wait a while, the worms will burrow into the centre of the mound, making separating easier.

Eventually, you will end up with a pile of compost next to a pile of worms. Return the worms to the bin and use the compost in the garden.

TIPS FOR A GOOD WORMERY

• The smaller you chop up food scraps,
the faster the worms will eat them.

• Collect the water (liquid fertiliser)
that drips out the bottom of the
bin by placing a plastic tray underneath.
You can empty this onto the garden.

• Remember that a wormery is a tiny ecosystem.
The only other living things you should
remove from your wormery are centipedes,
as they will eat baby worms and worm eggs.

• Shredded paper junk mail and cardboard from
cereal and pizza boxes make excellent bedding.

• Don't let your bin dry out.
This will kill the worms.

• Never handle worms with your bare hands.
The oils from your fingers will
clog their pores and suffocate them.

• Don't leave your worms
out in very cold weather.

WORMS LIKE...

… tea bags, coffee grounds, fruit, vegetable
peelings, egg shells, toilet and kitchen rolls,
hair, dust from the vacuum cleaner, cereals,
bread, green leaves and cow manure.

WORMS DON'T LIKE...

… meat, fish, cheese, baked beans,
rice, pasta, cooked potatoes, grass in
large amounts, and cat or dog poo.

A-MAZING MAZE

Johnny loves collecting things, but he's constantly losing his treasures around the house. In this maze are four of his favourite things: (1) a Penny Black stamp, (2) a blue teddy bear, (3) a model car and (4) a dinosaur egg. Begin at START and see if you can find the missing objects in the correct order, ending up in the kitchen. You cannot use the same route twice.

The answer is on page 60.

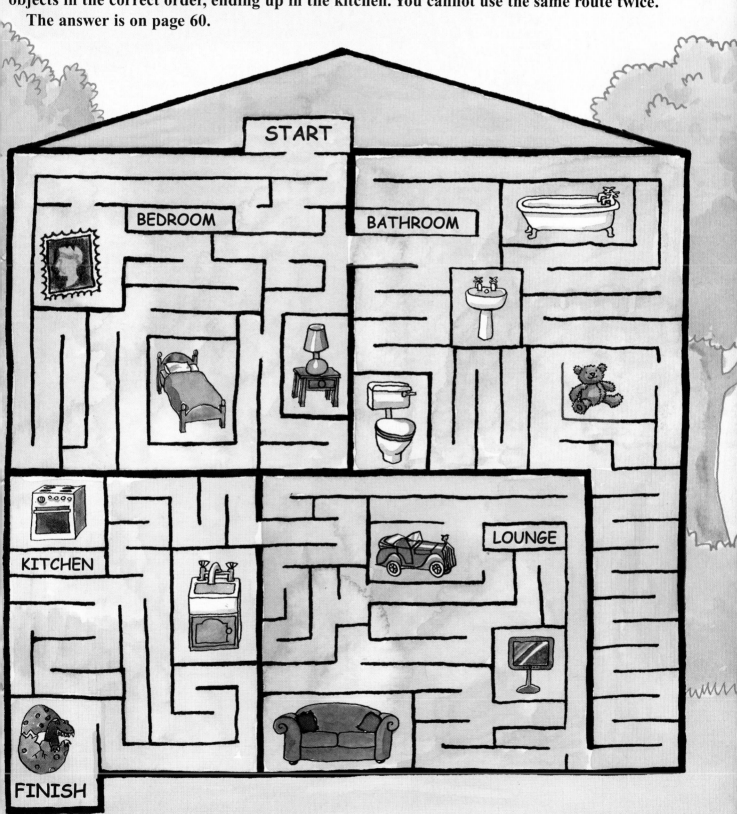

THE SECRETS TO
GOOD SPYING

Have you ever wondered what it's like to be a spy? Here are some things you can try out with your friends.

MASTERS OF DISGUISE

Good spies are able to disguise themselves, so that no one recognises them – not even their own mothers. The basic tools for a good disguise are false teeth, dark sunglasses, wigs, hats and clothes that you wouldn't normally wear. Most of these things can be found very cheaply at charity shops. You should also look around the shops at Halloween time for things like false teeth and wigs.

This boy is wearing a disguise. Can you work out which silhouette matches the picture? Answer on page 61.

Remember, a good disguise isn't just about clothes and props. Think of it as if you were preparing for a part on the stage. How would the old man that you've created walk? Would he use a cane? Would his voice be a bit weak, or a bit raspy? With time, you will create several different characters that you can become. The key is to keep each of them the same every time you assume the disguise.

A BOY OF MANY ACCENTS

Another way to change your identity is to experiment with different accents. For practice, try asking someone for directions, but speak with a foreign accent.

If the person asks where you are from, don't use a commonly known country like France, as they might start talking to you in perfect French. Try saying you are from Latvia, or Iceland, or better still, make up a country. How about Transruzinia or Abazistan? You can then make up a whole identity for yourself as a Transruzinian or Abazistani – a new name, where you grew up, how many brothers and sisters you have, where you go to school – the possibilities are endless.

YOU'RE LUCKY TO BE A BOY

Ever wondered why you were born a boy and not a girl? Probably not. And why wonder anyway? Just be glad, grateful and extremely relieved. Here are some reasons why it's good to be a boy.

You'll never have to wear high heels and you won't have to spend hours doing your hair and makeup.

Kick! *Foul!* *Run!* *Time out!*

You can talk endlessly about sport.

You will never be given anything pink, unless you ask for it.

You don't have to cry if you don't want to. Of course, if you want to, that's fine. You're human, too.

You can make rude noises and people will laugh and say, 'Boys will be boys'.

You can sit with your legs wide apart whenever you want.

You don't have to make small talk. You don't have to comment on how lovely your Auntie Jane's new hairdo is. If you want to sit quietly, you can do, you're a boy.

You rarely have to sit on toilet seats in public toilets.

JOKE TIME

Q. What's grosser than gross?
A. When you throw your underwear across the room and it sticks to the wall!
Q. What's grosser than that?
A. When you come back an hour later and it's moved up the wall one metre!

SUPERHERO YOU

Here's your chance to live out a superhero fantasy. Below is an unfinished story. You need to fill in the gaps by coming up with a word for each of the items in the story list. When you are done, use the words to fill in the gaps in the story in the order that they appear in the list. The only rule is – no peeking at the story until you've finished the list.

SUPERHERO STORY LIST

(1) Your own superhero name (2) your own superhero name, as per item 1 (3) your age
(4) a favourite activity (5) a sport (6) a real person (7) an animal, or bird (8) where you live
(9) an item of food (10) an object (11) the colour of your superhero outfit (12) your own superhero name, as per item 1 (13) an item of clothing (14) an amazing superhero skill (15) an animal, or bird, as per item 7
(16) a disgusting object (17) your own superhero name, as per item 1
(18) another superhero skill (19) an animal or bird, as per item 7 (20) a body part

_____1_____ SAVES THE DAY!

_____2_____ was an amazing superhero. Even though he was only _____3_____, he was very experienced and had long since given up wasting his time on _____4_____ and _____5_____.

One day, this superhero got a call from _____6_____ – he was desperately needed. Giant _____7_____ were taking over _____8_____, they were everywhere. They were eating all the _____9_____ and crushing all the _____10_____.

In a brilliant flash of _____11_____, superhero _____12_____ flew to the top of a building ready for action. He even had his _____13_____ on. First, he used his _____14_____ on the _____15_____. This made them angry and they fought back by throwing lots of _____16_____, but that didn't stop superhero _____17_____.

He _____18_____ the giant _____19_____ in the _____20_____ and they ran away crying, never to be seen again.   THE END

CREATE YOUR OWN SUPERHERO

Finish the superhero and his
arch enemy below by adding masks,
capes, boots, logos and weapons
and then colour them in.

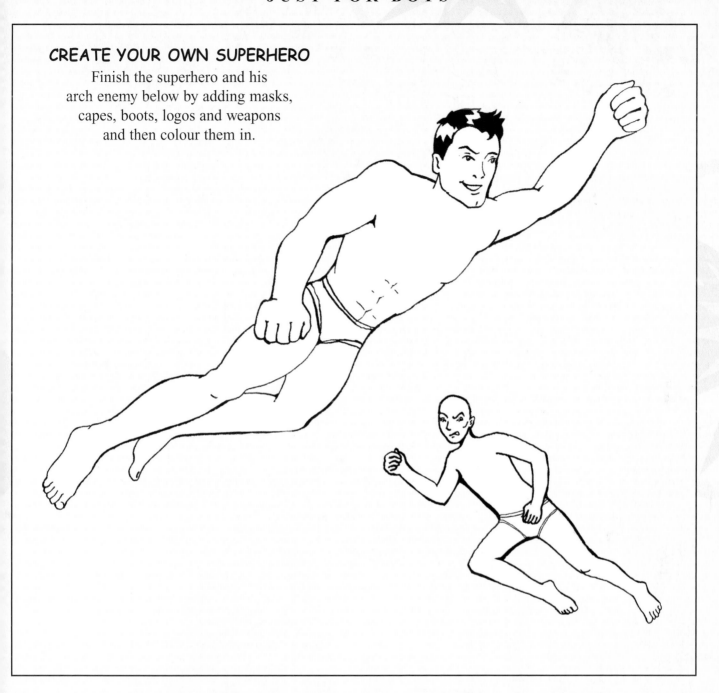

• S U P E R H U M A N •

MARATHON MONKS

The monks of Mount
Hiei in Kyoto, Japan,
must run up to 33
miles each night for
100 nights in a row, as
a way to reach
Enlightenment,
or 'oneness' with
the universe.

THE SADHUS OF INDIA

Many Sadhus, or Holy
Men, in India have made
it into the record books
for incredible feats
including: standing for
17 years, crawling for
870 miles and being
buried alive, sometimes
for three days.

SURVIVAL GUIDE

• PART TWO •

Using a compass and reading a map are two essential skills for survival in the field. It is important to be able to give clear directions and find something using a map. Here are some tips.

READING A COMPASS

The compass has four main (cardinal) points. These are North (N), South (S), East (E) and West (W). There are also intercardinal points. These are halfway between the cardinal points and are named for the points they lie between. They are Northeast (NE), Southeast (SE), Southwest (SW) and Northwest (NW).

There are eight more points on a compass. They are called the secondary intercardinal points. They lie halfway between the cardinal and intercardinal points. They are also named according to the points they lie between. The cardinal point comes first, then the intercardinal point. The first four are: North-northeast (NNE), East-northeast (ENE), East-southeast (ESE), South-southeast (SSE) and so on.

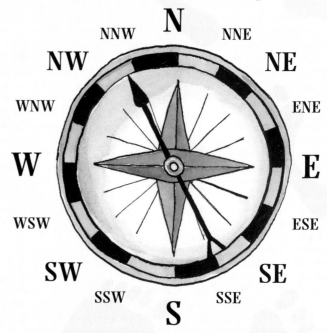

MAKING A COMPASS

If on a mission your pocket compass got damaged, don't panic. Here's how you can make one.

You will need: a thin needle – be careful of your fingers / a bar magnet – a fridge magnet will also do / a small piece of cork / a cup, or bowl of water.

Rub the needle over the magnet several times in one direction only, or leave the needle on the magnet overnight. Push the needle through a small piece of cork. Then place the needle and cork in a cup, or bowl of water. Watch the needle move until it stops. Where the needle points to should now be North. Give the needle a little push. If it moves back to where it was pointing before, you've made a compass.

JOKE TIME

Q. Why do cows wear bells?
A. Because their horns don't work!

TEST YOUR COMPASS READING SKILLS

See if you can work your way around this solar map. Begin by marking a cross with a pencil in the START square, then follow the directions in the box below, one by one, marking a cross in each square you land in. By the time you reach the FINISH, you should have used all the squares only once. Answer on page 61.

LIST OF DIRECTIONS

GO 5S, 3E, 1SW, 1E, 1S, 2W, 1N, 1W, 3S,
4E, 1N, 1NE, 4N, 1NE, 1S, 3E, 2S, 1NW, 2S,
2W, 1SE, 3S, 1NW, 3S, 5E, 1NW, 1E, 3N,
1SW, 1S, 2W, 2N, 1E, 1N, 1W, 1NE, 1E,
1SE, 5N, 1SW, 1N, 1NE, 1N, 3W, 1S, 1SE,
2W, 2N, 4W, 3S, 1NE, 2S, 3W, 2N, 1E, 2N, 1W

JOKE TIME

Q. What's brown and sticky?
A. A stick!

READING A MAP

A good map will have a key, or legend, which gives you all kinds of useful information. It tells you what the different symbols on a map mean and how many miles you need to go to get to your destination.

A detailed local map will provide you with all the information you need, from hostels and campsites to rivers, churches, footbridges, footpaths, fields and woods.

Remember, symbols will often mean different things on maps made in different countries.

FINDING A LOCATION

Most maps are divided into a grid of squares. These squares are a way to pinpoint a specific location. Look at the edges of a map. Along the top, at regular intervals, you will see letters starting with 'A'. Along the side, you will see numbers starting at '1'. Square A1 is therefore the top left square. Square B1 will be the next square on the right, while square B2 will be the square below, and so on.

SCALE

Every good map will include a scale to help you work out the distance you have to travel. The scale simply tells you what actual distance is represented on the map. For example, a scale of a centimetre to a mile means that every centimetre on the map represents an actual mile in distance.

CONTOUR LINES

On many maps, you will see thin, wavy lines called contour lines. These lines show you the height, or elevation, at that point of the ground above sea level. Follow a contour line on your map and you will see a number, like 140. This tells you how high the ground is. Check the key to see whether this is in metres or feet. If contour lines are far apart, the landscape around you should be fairly flat and even. If contour lines are close together, this means that the landscape is steep and hilly.

SCALE: 1 square = 3 km

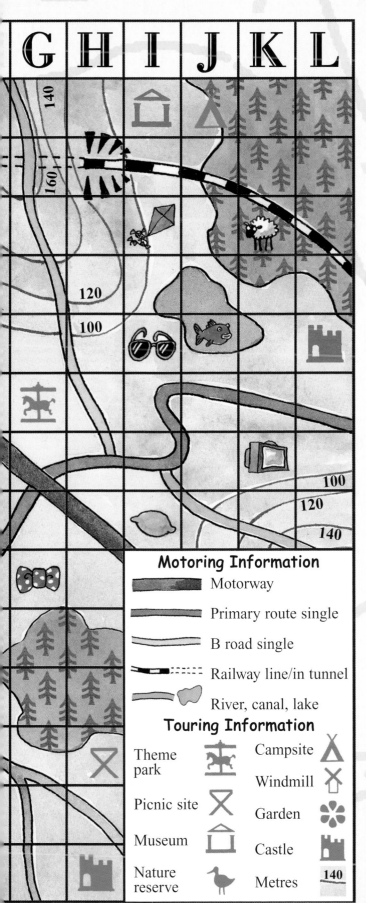

All answers can be found on page 61. Can you give the grid references for the following:
1. The 'red' castle.
2. The nature reserve.
3. The large fish.
4. The toilet.
5. The bicycle.
6. The sheep.
7. A pair of red and blue Y-fronts.

What can be found at the following grid references:
1. K7
2. H12
3. J1
4. A13
5. H14
6. C5
7. D6
8. B7
9. I5

Find the scale and work out the distance from:
1. The toilet to the bee.
2. The cup cake to the bow tie.
3. The 'red' museum to the lemon.
4. The nature reserve to the theme park.
5. The bee to the red and blue Y-fronts.
6. The 'blue' garden to the 'blue' castle.
7. The sheep to the TV.
8. The picnic site to the 'blue' castle.

What is the height of the land at the following points:
1. H4
2. D14
3. D5
4. A8

Use the clues and give the grid references for these objects:
1. You can watch TV here.
2. Avoid the angry bee here.
3. Long John Silver left his treasure here.
4. Get your eggs here.
5. Go for a trip under the water here.
6. You can fly a kite here.
7. You lost your yellow and blue Y-fronts here.
8. You can go fishing here.
9. You can get carrots here.

Motoring Information
Motorway

Primary route single

B road single

Railway line/in tunnel

River, canal, lake

Touring Information
Theme park

Picnic site

Museum

Nature reserve

Campsite

Windmill

Garden

Castle

Metres   140

MAKE AN
ANT FARM

Ever fancied being a myrmecologist and having your own formicarium? (By the way, this means, have you ever fancied becoming an ant expert with your own ant farm?)

To make an ant farm, you will need: a large, glass fish bowl, or a fish tank / a smaller bowl / some ants and some soil.

1. Place the smaller bowl upside down in the middle of the glass fish bowl, or tank. This ensures that the ants build their tunnels near the glass, so you can see them at work. If you don't do this, the ants may build their tunnels in the centre of the fish bowl/tank and then all you will see is lots of soil!

2. Fill the bottom of your fish bowl/tank with soil.

3. Now go into your garden – remember to take your ant farm with you. Look for ants. When you find some, gently start digging with a plastic spoon and transfer the ants and soil to your bowl/tank. Collect as many ants as you can.

4. Once you have your ants and soil, you may need to add some extra soil. The soil should be at least 5 cm from the top of the fish bowl/tank and it should be fairly tightly packed.

5. Although ants should not be able to climb up the glass walls of your container, you may want to add a lid, just in case. If you do use a lid, make sure that you punch a lot of small holes in it, so your ants can breathe. Now sit back and observe.

JOKE TIME

Q. What do you call an ant who skips out of school?
A. A tru-ant!

DID YOU KNOW?

- The largest ant colony is in Hokkaido, Japan. It is believed that there are over 300 million worker ants in the colony and over one million queen ants.
- A super colony of ants was discovered in 2002 that covered 3,728 miles under Europe.
- There are over 11,880 species of ant around the world.
- Ants can carry 10 to 20 times their own body weight.

LOOKING AFTER YOUR ANT FARM

Ants like to eat breadcrumbs, or bread dipped in sugar water. They also like small amounts of fruit and vegetables, but take care not to overfeed them.

Ants get most of their liquid needs from their food, but you can also add a little water to their diet. Every day, simply add some cotton wool soaked in water to your bowl or tank.

Avoid moving your bowl/tank too often, as movement may dislodge soil and the tunnels may collapse.

If you want to decorate your ant farm, add some miniature buildings or trees to the surface – these are available from model and hobby shops, or else plant grass seed on the surface.

NOTES AND WARNINGS

- Be very careful when selecting ants for your ant farm. Try to avoid ones that bite!

- If you are struggling to find ants in your area, then look into ordering ants from a specialist company. Check with your local hobby or pet shop.

ANSWER PAGE

IT'S A... BOYS' WORLD

Page 8: There are boys all over...

1. c, May 5th   **2.** c, pronounced 'Poykuh'
3. a   **4.** a, these boys become mahouts – elephant keepers   **5.** d   **6.** b   **7.** d   **8.** b, and he was only ten years old   **9.** b

Page 8: Flag Flurry

A = 4	B = 11	C = 7	D = 8	E = 3
F = 10	G = 17	H = 14	I = 1	J = 2
K = 20	L = 13	M = 9	N = 19	O = 5
P = 6	Q = 18	R = 16	S = 15	T = 12

PUZZLED?

Page 18: Road Rage

1 = E	2 = J	3 = T	4 = B	5 = L
6 = H	7 = A	8 = S	9 = Q	10 = F
11 = C	12 = O	13 = I	14 = D	15 = N
16 = K	17 = G	18 = M	19 = R	20 = P

Page 19: A Worm 'Wriddle'

There are 21 worms in the garden.

Page 19: Brain-Ache

1) The milkman fills the five litre jug and empties the contents into the three litre jug. The milk remaining in the five litre jug is exactly two litres.

2) The milkman fills the three litre jug and empties the contents into the five litre jug. He then fills the three litre jug again and continues to fill the five litre jug until it is full. There is precisely one litre left in the three litre jug.

Page 19: It's A Riddle

A cherry when it is blooming has no stone.
A chicken when it is in the shell has no bone.
The story of how I love you has no end.
A baby when it is sleeping doesn't cry.

BOOM-BANG-A-BANG!

Page 23: Pennies For Your Thoughts

Copper coins get dull over time because the copper reacts with air to form copper oxide. When you clean them in the solution, the acid from the vinegar dissolves the copper oxide and leaves your pennies bright and shiny. However, if you don't rinse the vinegar/salt solution from the pennies, the residue on the pennies will actually speed up the oxidisation process and this results in a layer of blue green copper oxide developing. This is a perfect way to make old-looking coins for a treasure hunt, for example.

CRACK THAT CODE

Page 24: A secret code can be anything...

The message is: So, you think you can crack this one, clever clogs?

Page 24: For another code, you could...

The message is: That one was easy, this one is much harder.

A-MAZING MAZE

Page 31: Johnny loves collecting things...

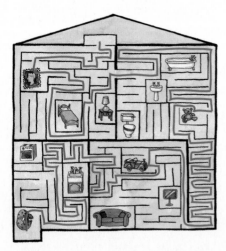

JOKE TIME

JOKE TIME

Q. What do you call a yeti in a phone box?
A. Stuck!

THE SECRETS TO GOOD SPYING

Page 32: This boy is wearing a...

Silhouette C matches the picture.

DO BOYS PLAY THAT?

Page 36: Boys play games in all parts...

1. True. For people in these countries, it's not always about winning, but about learning how to get on with each other.
2. True.
3. True. Bimbo is Italian for baby.
4. False. The game is actually called Chinese Chicken.
5. True.
6. True. Boys love to modify their tops to make them faster.
7. True. They usually write something really witty, like 'poo'.
8. False. But there is a game called 'King of the Hill' with the same rules.
9. True.
10. True.

TO CLEAN, OR NOT TO!

Page 42: John's idea of tidying...

Page 43: A Pile Of Y-Fronts

There are 31 Y-fronts in the pile.

ALMOST TRUE GHOST STORIES

Page 45: Ghost Hunt

There are 38 ghosts hiding on both pages.

ORIGAMI THIS

Page 47: Jack's thrown four...

Aeroplane A hit Dad, aeroplane B hit Jack's sister, aeroplane C hit Mum and aeroplane D hit the dog.

COOL AS A CREEPY-CRAWLY

Page 49: Where Did They Go?

There are 26 insects in the picture.

SURVIVAL GUIDE PART TWO

Page 55: Test Your Compass Reading Skills

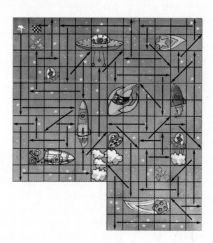

Page 57: Can you give the grid...

1. L5   2. D6   3. J5   4. A1   5. D8
6. K3   7. A14

Page 57: What can be found at...

1. a TV   2. a picnic site   3. a campsite
4. a museum   5. a castle   6. a hen
7. a nature reserve   8. a windmill   9. sunglasses

Page 57: Find the scale and work...

1. 12 miles   2. 21 miles   3. 24 miles   4. 12 miles
5. 33 miles   6. 18 miles   7. 15 miles   8. 9 miles

Page 57: What is the height of the...

1. 120 metres   2. 100 metres   3. 100 metres
4. 120 metres

Use the clues and give the...

1. K7   2. A4   3. D11   4. C5   5. D7
6. I3   7. C13   8. J5   9. C1